# KEYS
# TO A
# SOUND MIND

By

Dr. Shirley Christian

Keys to a Sound Mind
Copyright © January 2008
Shirley Christian Ministries
In Streams of His Grace
ISBN 978-0-6151-8974-1

www.shirleychristian.org

# WHY I WROTE THIS BOOK

God desires His beloved children to walk in His love, His power and soundness of mind, free of fear or torment of any kind. Sin and its effects are not to reign in our lives, nor should the enemy have any place in our lives. While we know that we will not escape tribulation, we also know that Jesus conquered the world, and we can find our peace in Him (see John 16:33). Divine attributes of love, power and a sound mind are made available to those in Christ Jesus. As with many of the blessings of God, we must possess and hold on to what is made available.

When the enemy begins to oppress a person's mind, the person sometimes believes that they have an evil spirit. Most often, it can be attributed to negative thoughts and beliefs. You cannot cast out something of this nature. You must overcome negative thoughts and emotions. God gives the victory through Jesus Christ! He gives grace to overcome.

The Bible encourages believers to receive the Word of God, believe the Word, speak the Word., and do the Word. We should hold on to the promises of God with "jaws of faith." Take the truth in this book and bite down on it with jaws of faith that hold it as with a vise grip. Do not be moved by feelings, thoughts or doubts that are not of God. Your doubts need to be doubted!

Keys to a Sound Mind was birthed out of affliction and inspired by the Word and the Spirit to help other believers possess what belongs to them through faith. Please read the book completely through in one sitting, then return to the beginning and daily meditate on the keys and the scriptures as you would a devotional book. You will increase as you persevere.

For God did not give us a spirit of fear but a spirit of power, love and a sound mind.  (2 Timothy 1:7)

This poor man cried, and the LORD heard and saved him
from all his troubles. The angel of the LORD encamps
around those who fear Him, and rescues them.
**(Psalm 34:6–7)**

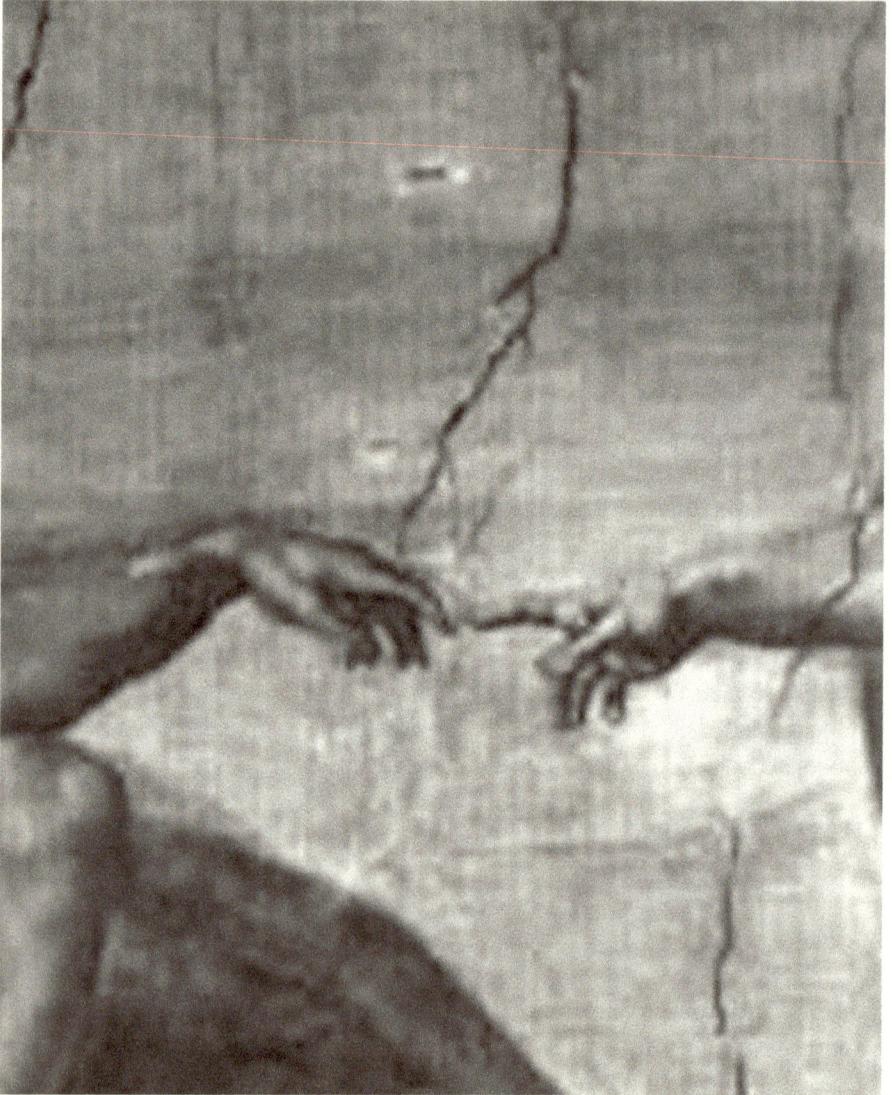

# TABLE OF CONTENTS

## Renew Your Mind On Your Right Standing With God

Through the faith of Jesus Christ, you have become the very righteousness of God. He now sees you in His own righteousness. You are "upright" before Him. You are able to stand before Him without fear, shame, guilt, or any sense of guilt from your past because of the blood of Christ Jesus. Your righteousness is an accomplished fact, Christ Jesus having paid the penalty for all sin, even though He lived without sin. Jesus bought with His own blood the contract that Satan held against us because of sin.

> *Jesus bought with His own blood the contract that Satan held against us because of sin.*

God takes no pleasure in those who draw back from Him (Hebrews 10:38). We are to approach the throne of grace as those who have been brought into the family of God in right relationship with Him, not as cowards (Hebrews 4:16, 10:38). We have confidence and bold access through Christ's blood (Ephesians 3:12, 2:13).

The thief on the cross beside Jesus did not draw back or hesitate to ask Jesus to "remember" Him. He boldly asked, not thinking on his own lack of righteousness, but on that which would come through the Lord's offering of Himself on the cross. To remember in Hebrew means to also act. Jesus assured the thief that he would be with Him in Paradise (Luke 23:42). You can also rely on His offering, and think on and speak

> *Faith is the instrument that you use to receive from God and also to stand against Satan*

about your righteousness in Christ, your right standing with God. Faith is the instrument that you use to receive from God and also to stand against Satan. Your faith will rise or fall with thoughts, beliefs, and confession of your righteousness in Christ Jesus.

### Scripture Meditation

God made this sinless man be a sin offering on our behalf, so that in union with him we might fully share in God's righteousness. (1 Corinthians 5:21 JNT)

## Bury The Past With The Old Man

Fill your mind with thoughts on your position in Christ. Refuse to accept any negative thoughts or feelings as to your past. Paul told the saints in Colossi, "You died and your life is hid with Christ in God" (Colossians 3:3). When baptism occurred, you died and came into contact with the very blood of Christ. In union with Him, you came up from the water a new creature. Paul exclaims, "Or are you unaware that all of us who were baptized into Christ Jesus were baptized into His death?" (Romans 6:3).

You are alive in Christ, a part of His spiritual body. You have been grafted into Him as a new branch, ready to blossom and bear fruit (see John 15). Since you have been made righteous, your mind should refuse sin-consciousness thoughts, and instead, maintain a state of righteousness-consciousness. If you have a thought of condemnation, it is not of God. Your own conscious will condemn you until you get right with God through repentance. But once you are right with God, refuse thoughts of condemnation. Replace them with righteous thoughts, right thoughts. You can have right ways of thinking or wrong ways of thinking. It is your choice. Solomon affirms, "The thoughts of the righteous are right" (Proverbs 12:5).

The Apostle Paul was a murderer and a persecutor of the church. Paul referred to himself as the "chief of all sinners" (1Timothy 1:15). After Jesus appeared to Paul, and he believed in Jesus, God sent a man to baptize Paul and lay hands on him to receive the Holy Spirit. Paul never looked back. He received revelation on his righteousness in Christ. He confessed, "Brethren, I count not myself to apprehended but one thing, forgetting those things which are behind . . ." (Philippians 3:13a). This former sinner is credited with having written two-thirds of the New Testament through the Holy Spirit's inspiration.

> *Changing your words can change your thoughts and your feelings*

Changing your words about your past will change your feelings and future. You will not be able to think bad thoughts and speak at the same time. Try it.

### Scripture Meditation

Therefore if any person is [ingrafted] in Christ (the Messiah) he is a new creation (a new creature altogether); the old [previous moral and spiritual condition] has passed away. Behold, the fresh and new has come! (2 Corinthians 5:17 AMP)

# A Renewed Mind Has A New Attitude

Your entire inner being, your soul (consisting of your mind, will and emotions), and your spirit, is extremely sensitive to what you choose to think and speak about; i.e., your mind and your spirit will conform to what you tell it about yourself. If you dwell on negative thoughts and do not limit the world's influence in your life, then you will conform to the world—its ungodliness. If you meditate on and speak words consistent with who you have become in Christ, then your soul and spirit will align with Christ. Your attitude, either joyful and expectant or negative, will determine your altitude emotionally. It also tells those around you to what degree you are representing God.

> *You choose to be transformed by changing your thoughts and your words, based on what the Word of God says about you.*

You choose to be transformed by changing your thoughts and your words, based on what the Word of God says about you. God's plan is that you will one day be made like Christ, in not only your spirit, but your soul and body as well. To be conformed means to be molded or fashioned according to a pattern. Paul writes:

> For those whom He foreknew, He also predestined to become conformed to the image of His Son, so that He would be the firstborn among many brethren. (Romans 8:29)

God sometimes allows the trials in life in order to dredge up things you need to see, and which need to be removed from your life. Allow God to help you remove anything that does not conform to Christ's image in you. God is the potter who molds you as you stay on His sculpting wheel, shaped by the Word and Spirit of God.

## Scripture Meditation

Do not be conformed to this world (this age), [fashioned after and adapted to its external, superficial customs], but be transformed (changed) by the [entire] renewal of your mind [by its new ideals and its new attitude] . . . (Romans 12:2a AMP)

9

## Your Internal Belief System is a Key to Your Wholeness

We often take for granted that others experienced loving and secure environments as they grew up. Yet most people do not have enough security in Christ to be vulnerable about their lives. Most wear a mask that they present to the world. How we view others and ourselves as adults is greatly determined by how our parents treated us—either with love and respect or low regard and minimal care. Below is a chart demonstrating a fear-based system of belief and a love-based system of belief.

| Love-Based Belief System | | | |
|---|---|---|---|
| My parents gave **unconditional love**, **approval, and acceptance to me**, and created an environment in which I felt **secure.** | I believe that God is loving, patient, and good. **God is glad.** | I possess a healthy self-concept, sense of **security,** and wholesome self-esteem. **I am glad**. | *I prefer* or **want** to be accepted, but if not, I am OK. Even if I make a mistake, **I am OK** |
| **Fear-Based Belief System** | | | |
| My parents neglected, rejected, abandoned, and condemned me, and created an environment in which I felt insecure, **broken and flawed.** | I believe that God is demanding, impatient, if I mess up, ready to zap me at any moment. **God is mad.** | I possess an unhealthy self-concept, a sense of being **insecure,** and I have to earn approval for self-worth. **I am sad.** | *I have* to be accepted, or I am not OK. *I have* to perform well, or **I am not OK** |

**If you see that your self-worth is based on the Fear-Based System, then you definitely need to dwell on the very next day's devotional, as well as reread all the devotions daily to rewire your sense of security in Christ.**

# The Science of Rewiring Your Brain for Right Decisions

We may receive 11 million bits of information a second into our brain through our five senses: touch, taste, sound, smell, and sight. Information is then reduced through a series of filters to manageable amounts. The brain's *thalamus* acts like a filter for this information. Acting much like a central switching station or junction box, scientists pose that the thalamus sends the information to other parts of the brain responsible for processing it. Eighty percent more information is brought back to the thalamus from other areas of the brain from stored data, and is not necessarily based on *reality.*

The thalamus, seeking to protect us from pain, has the ability to bypass our own conscious decision-making and make decisions based on perceptions it has stored from an age at which trauma occurred. *Arrested development* is found in someone who experienced abuse at a young age and failed to receive healing from it. The definition for it is "a developmental disorder that occurs at some stage in a child's development, often retarding the development psychologically or physically" (Wikepedia).

The thalamus is physically and emotionally "wired" to filter information related to a "perceived" threat, which it perceives as traumatic; i.e., it has matching criteria, or related emotional criteria such as created from the childhood wound. While the person may mature physically, he/she retains a childlike perspective on certain areas of life and never progresses beyond that age in certain areas of decision-making. For example, trauma from abuse at an age when we were more parentally directed in our decisions, and not cognitively making them, leaves a wound that acts through the thalamus to wire our brains to avoid similar pain again.

You might think of trauma as something producing a "brain injury," a term derived from my prayers on establishing wholeness in others. Thus, if someone has been wounded at an early age, when information comes into the thalamus, the brain receives information filtered through a perception of brokenness. A fear and shame-based belief system develops from early wounds, producing low self-esteem, and an unholy pride, causing one to perceive his/herself as lacking, broken or flawed. This person never becomes whole because of fear, and a self-centered outlook. Typically such sufferers are performance driven, addictive personalities, not realizing their motive is gaining approval. Some sufferers internalize everything, blocking out problems or difficult situation. Frozen emotions and paralysis results. It is like stuffing something down inside us that will cause us to be driven in areas of decision-making and life issues. Stuffed emotions, internalized difficulties, will like most damaged emotions, result in physical sickness.

If two out of four women were sexually abused as children, and men abused as well, and others suffer from other early childhood wounds such as rejection or abandonment, then we have many setting in churches suffering from arrested development. Most importantly, these adults are still hurting.

The way to heal many emotional issues and produce cognitive decision-making is by *rewiring* one's brain with truth—the Word, thus creating new perceptions for the thalamus and brain areas receiving and filtering information. Healing results in the ability to see reality. For example, a child is abused at ten years of age, and as an adult, the thalamus filters all perceptions from the outside through that filter of abuse, and makes decisions based on that stage of life. They are "programmed" to perceive future events as traumatic. **The Word of God, mediated on, and affirmed through Word-filled affirmations (confessions of the truth), will eventually rewire the brain and bring the person to wholeness (maturity)**, with the ability to make decisions using the area of brain more suitable for wise decisions.

"Rewiring," may not occur overnight, but diligence will always produce results. The Holy Spirit, through the anointing, can go to the core and bring light and truth, so that the brain injury is healed, and thought processes begin to function properly. However, lasting change must be pursued through rewiring the brain (renewing the mind) to the knowledge of God's great love and reconciliation through Christ. When we truly being to understand that God loves us, we have value to God, and are safe, we can begin to mend.

### Scripture Meditation

Those who come to God must believe that He is, and that He cares enough to respond, reward, and restore those who seek Him. . (Hebrews 11:6 paraphrase)

# Changing Your Internal Image

Your inner self receives a new nature when you accept Jesus Christ, but your internal image of yourself must be transformed to align with this new nature. Satan will attack this inner image or portrait, but your must continue to allow God to bring your inner image, what you believe about yourself, into alignment with your new nature. Accept who you are in Christ, and more importantly, who He is in you, letting your mind and spirit understand its new position, new ideals and new attitude. You will begin to see and be transformed to the perfect will of God. Just like a caterpillar is changed into a butterfly, your inner transformation, a metamorphosis, takes place as you meditate on and speak the Word of God.

Only the Word of God is able to keep your mind and spirit in line. The writer of Hebrews says,

> For the word of God is living and active and sharper than any two-edged sword, and piercing as far as the division of soul and spirit, of both joints and marrow, and able to judge the thoughts and intentions of the heart. (Hebrews 4:12)

Study and speak the Word. Say to yourself daily; "Body line up with my soul; soul line up my spirit; spirit line up with the Holy Spirit." Put on Christ— bring to mind that Christ is in you. Your outer conforming follows as you begin to act in accordance to what you believe about yourself, fashioned into the very pattern of the original, Christ Jesus. Consider what Paul explains, "But we have this treasure in clay vessels, that the exceeding greatness of the power may be of God, and not from ourselves" (2 Corinthians 4:7). Yes, in us, resides this glory!

## Scripture Meditation

Do not be conformed to this world (this age), [fashioned after and adapted to its external, superficial customs], but be transformed (changed) by the [entire] renewal of your mind [by its new ideals and its new attitude so that you may prove [for yourselves] what is the good and acceptable and perfect will of God, even the thing which is good and acceptable and perfect [in His sight for you]. (Romans 12:2 AMP)

13

## Changing Your Internal Image
## By Daily Confession and Meditation

**Confess daily**: God's Word is true, and it is the source of understanding God's authority in my life. It tells me that God loves me with an everlasting love. God loves me so much that He sent His Son into the world to demonstrate His love and reconcile me to Himself eternally.

Who I am is not about my past. It does not consist of my past failures or successes, and what others did to me. I am glad to be who I am, and I am not thinking I would be happier if I could be like someone else or perform like someone else. I refuse to compete with others or envy their lives. As a new creation in Christ, made righteous by His sacrifice, I have a sense of personal value that is totally unrelated to my performance or others rejection or acceptance of me.

Being successful does not equate to self-esteem for me. Further, my self-esteem is not based on the opinions of others (including relatives) or society. It brings me pleasure to do well, but I see it as a result of my security and stability in Christ. When I fail, and all do, it does not cause me to feel rejection, shame, or lack of approval. I refuse to feel rejection if others do not accept or approve of me—I refuse to be dominated by others' opinions of me. I do not have to please people to be accepted, nor do I manipulate others to get approval or acceptance. I am totally accepted in Christ, my Savior, secure in Him. I am hid in God with Christ.

I desire to love others as Christ loved me, and I desire to be pleasing to others, but not to receive approval or acceptance—just to honor and love others. I enjoy being me, and I respect myself; in fact, I have a wholesome love and respect for myself. I am unique, and I possess gifts and abilities that I desire to use to contribute to others—I find fulfillment in serving my Lord and His people. I am free to be thankful, and I desire to honor God, who loves me so very much.

## Scripture Meditation

Do not be conformed to this age, but be transformed by the renewing of your mind, so that you may discern what is the good, pleasing, and perfect will of God. (Romans 12:2 HCSB)

## Maintain A Fresh Mental and
## Spiritual Attitude


What happens to you in life is not as important as your attitude about it, how you respond to life. Your attitude is often affected by your emotional well-being. Set your emotional thermostat to a higher faith level by feeding on the Word of God, which renews your mind. Refuse to allow your emotions be moved by circumstances. Circumstances can change but the stability of the Word of God will not.

Many successfully avoid roller coaster emotions by maintaining a God-consciousness. Acknowledge that the Greater One lives in you (1 John 4:4). What attitude would He be most pleased with in all circumstances? I would say, "Love, joy, and peace." Paul wrote to the Philippians, "Not that I speak from want, for I have learned to be content in whatever circumstances I am" (Philippians 4:11). Keep in mind that he wrote this Epistle in a Roman prison. Peace is a great umpire for determining whether we are in faith or not.

Music will also help your attitude, fortitude, and change your countenance. It has the ability to bypass your mind and penetrate into your being. Take Paul's advice, "Be filled with the Spirit, speaking Psalms, hymns, spiritual songs and making melody in your heart to God" (Ephesians 5:19). You cannot praise God in music and stay down at the same time. The Psalmist exhorts worshippers in two Psalms that praise looks good on them. It will put a smile on your face and on God's. He will move you to dance and sing, and you will experience His deliverance. David sang, "You have turned my mourning into dancing for me. You have removed my sackcloth, and clothed me with gladness" (Psalm 30:11). "This poor man cried, and the LORD heard him, and saved him out of all his troubles" (Psalm 34:6).

## Scripture Meditation

And be constantly renewed in the spirit of your mind [having a fresh mental and spiritual attitude]. (Ephesians 4:23 AMP)

## Stop Delusion

No longer allow deception in your life. You were once conformed to the world by behaving just like those in the world. You did not know that you were being deceived and enslaved by the enemy. Your indulgence was based on your old nature of sin. Be done with it, strip it off, and identify with your new nature. Put away anything that does not accurately reflect your new nature. Sin seems enjoyable, but it is deceiving. Sin will always end in pain for you and whoever else it effects. Take this advice,

> My son, give attention to my words; Incline your ear to my sayings. Do not let them depart from your sight; Keep them in the midst of your heart. For they are life to those who find them And health to all their body. (Proverbs 4:20-22)

You will enjoy more of the life of God, maintain health, and have a renewed mind by purposing to have a constant flow of the Word of God before the gates of your eyes, ears, heart, and mouth. The Word creates a new image, in your mind and spirit of the real you, the one being conformed to the image of Christ. Paul groans, "My little children, of whom I am again in travail until Christ be formed in you" (Galatians 4:19).

> *Have a constant flow of the Word of God before the gates of your eyes, ears, heart, and mouth.*

Government agents learn to spot counterfeit bills by studying the original ones. Learn to recognize truth based on the Word of God, and stop Satan's deceptions in your life. You must meditate on Truth, fellowship with the Spirit of Truth, and reverence the God of Truth.

### Scripture Meditation

Strip yourselves of your former nature [put off and discard your old unrenewed self] which characterized your previous manner of life and becomes corrupt through lusts and desires that spring from delusion. (Ephesians 4:22 AMP)

## Make a Quality Decision

True righteousness and holiness are based on the character of God. You have learned that He made you righteous, giving you the ability to stand before Him without any sense of guilt, shame or cowardice. This new nature that He gave you is in His very image. Through deception, Eve led her man Adam, the first man who was created in God's image, to lose his right standing with God. Christ Jesus has won back your righteousness for you, giving you a new God-like nature. Your spirit has been regenerated; now alive for the first time.

Begin to say what God says about you,

I pray that your participation in the faith may become
effective through knowing every good thing that is in us
for the glory of Christ. (Philemon 1:6 HCSB)

This verse tells us that when we acknowledge the good things in us in Christ Jesus, our faith will be communicated effectively. It will begin to work! Choose to acknowledge Christ in you, His gifts and His calling. Remember to align your thoughts and your words to recognize His wisdom, righteousness and holiness as a part of your nature. Reject thoughts that are not worthy of your new nature. Make a quality decision to put on the new nature; the real you, which is "created in righteousness and holiness of the truth" (Ephesians 4:24).

> *Remember to align your thoughts and your words to recognize His wisdom, righteousness, and holiness as a part of your nature.*

You cannot change the choices you made yesterday that put you where you are today, but you can choose to make right choices today and change tomorrow's outcome. Your past is merely a stepping stone to your future. Walk out of the past and into the grand future prepared for you. This one decision is pivotal in advancing to a new level.

## Scripture Meditation

And put on the new nature (the regenerate self) created in God's image, [Godlike] in true righteousness and holiness. (Ephesians 4:24 AMP)

## Your Behavior Will Be Consistent With Your
## Internal Image of Yourself

Most of us think in pictures. When you describe something, you are creating an image in your mind's eye. Words create images, or visions. Create an image in your mind and spirit of who you are in Christ, and then live it out. You are to live out of your being, the real you, one who has recognized Christ's Lordship. The Apostle Paul exhorted believers in Ephesus to walk (to fall in line much as with a military command) as befitted their new divine nature and calling.

Images are created, much like a photograph or a painting is produced. As you speak and meditate on your new identity in union with Christ, you are adding more to the image in your mind and spirit, creating a masterpiece. David, the shepherd boy who became king, created a vision when he faced Goliath, the Philistine giant that he killed. David described his own earlier victories, and told Goliath exactly what his fate would be as he ran toward him armed with a slingshot, five stones, and the faith that God was with him. David said,

> You come against me with a dagger, spear and sword, but I come against you in the name of the LORD of Hosts, the God of Israel's armies--you have defied Him . . .the battle is the LORD's. He will hand you over to us. (1 Samuel 17:45, 47)

Notice that the battle is the Lord's, but David showed up to fight, and mostly with his mouth! He called his giant dead, then killed and beheaded him. Knowing God is on our side, we should have such confidence. Paul cries, "And such confidence have we through Christ in God" (2 Corinthians 3:4). David recognized the Lord of Hosts was on his side. God is on your side as well. The Psalmist confidently sings, "The LORD *is* on my side; I will not fear: what can man do unto me?" Psalm 118:6). Live worthy of Him in great confidence.

### Scripture Meditation

. . . walk (lead a life) worthy of the [divine] calling to which you have been called [with behavior that is a credit to the summons to God's service living as becomes you] (Ephesians 4:1AMP) .

# Act On The Truth That You Know

Jesus said, "I am the Way, the Truth and the Life" (John 14:6). Therefore, He spoke the truth. He sent the Spirit of Truth to be with us and in us (John 14:17), in order to know the things freely given to us by God (1 Corinthians 2:12). You were freely given His new nature, eternal life, and everything pertaining to life and godliness (2 Peter 1:3). Knowing you have received the Truth, live your life accordingly. Dishonesty is a contradiction in what you know and what you do and say, and it will cause disharmony within you and those in the body of Christ. Dishonesty includes withholding information. The sages call it "stealing the mind." When we only tell a piece of the truth, or tell an outright lie (often to make us look better to others), we withhold what someone has a right to know, and steal from them. Fear is often the cause of dishonesty and thus dis-ease within—fear of not measuring up to someone expectations or our own.. Walk in truth—John said, "I have no greater joy than this: to hear that my children are walking in the truth" (3 John 1:4).

As a new creature in Christ, upright before God, endued with His very nature, you are freed to live godly. You have been "created in the likeness of God in righteousness and holiness of the truth" (Ephesians 4:24). You have stripped off the old worldly nature and put on the new self by meditating on and speaking the Word of Truth to yourself—bringing to mind who lives in you. With a constant inflow of Truth in your mind and spirit, you will act in accordance with your transformation. Reject any thought or action that does not line up with this truth about your new life in Christ. Remember that obedience is not only in words, but also in action. Keep discord out and harmony in by speaking rightly. David sang, "If I regard iniquity in my heart, the Lord will not hear me" (Psalm 66:18).

We love and fear God; therefore, we love what He loves and hate what He hates. Listen to God: ". . . I will teach you the fear of the LORD. Keep your tongue from evil and your lips from deceitful speech"(Psalm 34:11,13 HCSB).

## Scripture Meditation

Assuming that you have really heard Him and been taught by Him, as [all] Truth is in Jesus [embodied and personified in Him]. (Ephesian 4:21 AMP)

# No Longer Live as a Child

One of the enemy's chief devices against believers is deception. He would like for you to swallow every new thought he feeds you. He would like for you to believe that God is not faithful to His Word, and that your past or present mistakes have disqualified you for abundant life. He would like for you to follow a different gospel, one of condemnation. Tell him, "No." If your thoughts do not line up with what God has said about you, then they are the enemy's lies. Replace them with God's thoughts of your right standing before Him and His plan for your life. Jeremiah wrote, "I know the plans I have for you, plans for a future and a hope, not for calamity" (Jeremiah 29:11).

God has not given up on us, and we should not give up on Him. Stay on His side. Do not believe lies about God or yourself. Speak truth and live truth. Even after King David committed adultery with Bathsheba and murdered her husband, he repented, God forgave him, and David was able to remain "a man after God's heart" (1 Samuel 13:14).

God's very nature includes forgiveness. He is holy and wants to bring us to Himself; therefore, He made us holy through His Son. The penalty for sin is death, but God paid it for us in order to reconcile us to Himself. He sent His Son as a substitute to give Himself for us. We are forgiven because of the blood of Christ, through Whom we have been brought near to God (see 2 Corinthians 5:18-19). We have peace with God , being acquitted of sin—justified (Romans 5:1). We access this grace through faith (Romans 5:2). Paul tells the Corinthian believers, "But you were washed, you were sanctified, you were justified in the name of the Lord Jesus Christ and by the Spirit of our God" (1 Corinthians 6:11).

## Scripture Meditation

. . . no longer be children, tossed (like ships) to and fro between chance gusts of teaching and wavering with every changing wind of doctrine,... Rather let our lives lovingly express truth (in all things, speaking truly, dealing truly, living truly). . . (Ephesians 4:14-15 AMP)

# Grow Up!

You have believed in Jesus Christ and received the truth. Your life will take on more meaning when you really "know what you know," and live out of that increased illumination of the Scriptures. As you continue to meditate on the truth and speak the truth, the Spirit of truth will bring more revelation to you, and you will actually receive in your spirit increased illumination of what you thought you already understood. Solomon wrote, "For thou wilt light my lamp" (Proverbs 18:28). The searchlight of the Spirit will reveal the deeper things of God. "The spirit of man *is* the lamp of the Lord, searching all the inward parts of the belly" (Proverbs 20:27). You have the anointing of the Holy Spirit on the inside to show you and teach you all things (see 1 John 2:27).

Emotions are a part of our nature—but emotions can rule a person not submitted to the Spirit of God. When emotions from offense or deception threaten to take over your otherwise sensible nature, speak the Word—bring them into subjection according to truth. Speak truth as long as necessary to bring unruly thoughts and emotions into conformance to your new nature. Instead of dwelling on wrong thoughts, rejoice, in fact, "consider it all joy" (James 1:2).

When you come to know Christ Jesus, you begin to grow up into all He is—remember, what you behold, you will become. You are entirely enfolded in the love of Christ, and rooted and grounded in the love of Christ (Ephesians 3:17), and able to comprehend and live as He lived in love, not as a selfish and self-willed child who is void of understanding. Tell yourself you are enfolded in His love and that you are growing up! Stop thinking and speaking in childish ways! Do not whine, complain, pout, or indulge in self-pity, which is sin. Instead, speak the Word so as to build up your faith, and believe God for the ability to hold your head up high. Paul wrote to the church at Corinth, "When I was a child I used to speak as a child; when I became a man, I did away with childish things" (1 Corinthians 13:11). Put away all that would hinder your maturity and grow into some "measure of the stature of the fullness of Christ" (Ephesians 4:13).

## Scripture Meditation

Enfolded in love, let us grow up in every way and in all things into Him who is the head, (even) Christ (the Messiah, the Anointed One) (Ephesians 4:15 AMP). Until we all attain to the unity of the faith, and the knowledge of the Son of God, to a mature man, to a measure of the stature of the fullness of Christ. (Ephesians 4:13 AMP)

## Understand and Live in God's Favor

Settle it in your mind and spirit: God is not mad at you; He is so very mad about you! God is not holding anything against you. In fact, you have been restored to the favor that He intended for His creatures. When you received the Lord Jesus, you came into harmony with His divine purpose. You have right standing before Him. Because He loved us, God made Christ to be a sin offering for us, and take the penalty due us (Romans 3:23-24). God then justified us in Christ, meaning that He declared us righteous and reconciled us to Him. Reconciliation means fellowship, peace and oneness with Him (see Romans 5:1, 2 Corinthians 5:18-19).

You can meditate on and speak to yourself of the favor that God has given you. Knowing this favor, His gifts, His goodness and kindness towards us, we are free to live a life of fellowship with Him. Christ has removed any sense of unworthiness or guilt, but we must lay hold of His favor to enjoy it. Let this fact of His divine favor transform your daily expectations. Begin each day expecting favor to unfold in your life.

To be in Christ means that we also get to experience His favor. Favor comes in the package of redemption—reconciliation with God. The Lord stood in His hometown synagogue and proclaimed a series of scriptures that He came to fulfill. God sent Him " to proclaim the year of the Lord's favor " (Luke 4:19 HCSB). The year of the Lord's favor is

> *Begin each day expecting favor to unfold in your life*

called "Jubilee." Jesus is our Jubilee. Jubilee is when freedom, restoration, debt cancellation, and the free favor of God flow profusely. Enjoy the favor of righteousness and righteous living: David wrote, "For You, LORD, bless the righteous one; You surround him with favor like a shield" (Psalm 5:12).

## Scripture Meditation

So we are Christ's ambassadors, God making His appeal as it were through us. We [as Christ's personal representatives] beg you for His sake to lay hold of the divine favor [now offered you] and be reconciled to God. (2 Corinthians 5:20 AMP)

## Stand Against the Enemy's Deceptions

You received the grace of God when you received Christ Jesus. If you do not grasp the full understanding of God's grace at work in you, then you will not live in its full potential. Do not "receive His grace in vain" (2 Corinthians 6:1). As you meditate on and speak to yourself about God's goodness, poured out on us through Christ, you will begin to live out of that knowledge and not be as subject to the world's pull and the enemy's deceptions. You act from a place of victory instead of defeat. The Lord's grace will strengthen and keep you. Paul advised his son in the faith, "Therefore my son, be strong in the grace of the Lord Jesus" (2 Timothy 2:1).

Grace is God's empowerment, favor, gifts, blessings, lovingkindness—faithfulness to covenant, and His willingness to use His power and ability on your behalf. According to James, the Lord's half-brother and Bishop of the Jerusalem Church, grace is also the power of God that he gives to you to overcome evil tendencies (James 4:6 AMP). His grace is sufficient to strengthen and keep you in every circumstance. The Lord said to Paul, "My grace is sufficient for you

> *Grace is God's empowerment, favor, gifts, blessings, lovingkindness—faithfulness to covenant, and His willingness to use His power and ability on your behalf*

(2Corinthians 12:9). He will tabernacle over you. Paul resolves to boast in his own weakness, "that the power of Christ might rest upon me" (2 Corinthians 12:10).

The primary way to overcome deception, and change your thoughts is to replace them. Either give yourself new thoughts from the Word, or speak the Word and thoughts and emotions follow. Take a scripture and meditate on it—repeat it over and over, think about its application, and recite it aloud. Act in accordance with the Word, and if you do it consistently, then you will also change your destiny in line with God's plan for your life.

## Scripture Meditation

. . . we beg of you not to receive the grace of God in vain [that merciful kindness by which God exerts His holy influence on souls and turns them to Christ, keeping and strengthening them—do not receive it to no purpose]. (2 Corinthians 6:1 AMP)

23

## Put God's Thoughts In Your Mind and Spirit

If you could have one key to success, to abundant living, to wisdom, to prosperity, then would you agree to use this key? The Lord gave such a key to Joshua (and to us). It is found in meditating and speaking the Word of God day and night. God told Joshua to keep the Word in His heart and mouth at all times so that he could do the Word of God and succeed. The Word will cut through unbelief, unsound reasonings, and layers of doubt to produce soundness of mind. The writer of Hebrews reminds us:

> For the word of God is living, and active, and sharper than any two-edged sword, and piercing even to the dividing of soul and spirit, of both joints and marrow, and is able to discern the thoughts and intentions of the heart. Heb 4:12

Joshua is chronicled as a leader and conqueror. Follow the same command God gave Joshua, and you will have a storehouse of knowledge and wisdom, and be empowered to live out of your inward revelation. This will create success in every area of your life.

It pleases God when we hide His Word in our hearts (Psalm 119:11). It makes His job easier. What you put into your mind and spirit will be a source for Him to use to bring revelation for your success. Cooperate with the Holy Spirit by feeding your spirit the Word. Solomon writes, "How much better it is to get wisdom than gold! And to get understanding is to be chosen above silver" (Proverbs 16:16). When God offered King Solomon anything Solomon desired, he chose wisdom. Success, riches and honor follow wisdom (see 2 Chronicles 1:11).

### Scripture Meditation

This book of the law shall not depart from your mouth, but you shall meditate on it day and night, so that you may be careful to do according to all that is written in it; for then you will make your way prosperous, and then you will have success. (Joshua 1:8)

24

# Dislodge Feelings of Disappointment & Discouragement
## With God's Thoughts

Your expectations of people and life will at times produce a sense of disappointment and discouragement, if you allow it. You must drop such feelings or you will be giving place to the devil. Many open the door to depression in their lives by dwelling on disappointments or discouragement. Know that people are not perfect and will inflict emotional pain on others. Exercise your God-given discipline and self-control, and replace thoughts of disappointment and discouragement with God's thoughts. Speaking the Word will help change your emotions rapidly. Read the Word, meditate on the Word, pray, casting your cares on Him, and fix your mind on God's thoughts and on heavenly things. Take Paul's advice,

> Whatever things are true, honorable, just, pure, lovely, of good report, of any virtue, of any praise, think about these things. (Philippians 4:8 paraphrase).

When a band of Amalekites raided David's camp, they took David's family and those of his men captive. His men were so distressed that they threatened to stone David. He could have become depressed, but instead he "strengthened himself in the Lord" and became victorious (1 Samuel 30:6). David sought God for direction and pursued the raiders. He and his men overtook them and brought back the captives. David sent the plunder from his raid to the elders in Israel, men who were influential in seeing David assume the throne of Israel. God is a God of restoration and reward. Mediate on His greatness and goodness.

You cannot help but rejoice when you meditate on the risen Christ, His place of honor in Heaven, and the things God has prepared for those who love Him in Heaven. God has laid up treasures for us. Paul writes, "Eye has not seen, and ear has not head, and it has not entered into the heart of man, all that God has prepared for those who love him" (1Corinthians 2:9).

## Scripture Meditation

Since you are seated above in Christ at the right hand of God, set your heart on things above. Then set continually your mind on things above. (Colossians 3:1, 3 paraphrase)

# Change Your Thoughts, and You Will Change Your Life

Wise people keep their minds occupied with things of the Spirit, and their purpose, their goals and vision. As you meditate on these things, your spirit will team up with the Holy Spirit and create your future. You will live with a sense of urgency and destiny when you set goals with the help of the Holy Spirit. Follow what God told Habakkuk,

> Record the vision and inscribe it on tablets, that the one who reads it may run. For the vision is yet for the appointed time; it hastens toward the goal and it will not fail. Though it tarries, wait for it; for it will certainly come, it will not delay. (Habakkuk 2:2-3)

Purpose and vision are like magnates that will bring into your life all that you need to fulfill the destiny that God has appointed for you. Whatever your vision, good or bad, you will achieve. Proverbs shows us: "For as he thinks in his heart, so is he" (Proverbs 23:7); and "As in water face answers to face, so the heart of man answers to man" (Proverbs 27:19). What you hold in your heart is a reflection of who you are. Believe God for the best. God promises to fulfill the desires of your heart when He is your primary focus. King David wrote and sang, "Delight yourself in the Lord, and He will give you the desires of your heart" (Psalm 37:4). To delight means to be moldable and teachable—and you are at no risk then to act on the desires of your heart. He puts His own desires in you. Live purposefully and accurately (see Ephesians 5:15).

Change your thoughts and change your life. You will either master your thoughts or they will master you! If you do not have a vision for your destiny on which to meditate and speak, pray and ask God. Also, attend a church with a big vision and it will rub off on you.

## Scripture Meditation

Look carefully then how you walk! Live purposefully and worthily and accurately, not as the unwise and witless, but as wise (sensible, intelligent people). (Ephesians 5:15 AMP)

26

# You Have the Mind of Christ

Jesus Christ repeatedly spoke of doing His Father's will, speaking His Father's words and doing His Father's works. He gave us the ability to be in this same close communion, such that we are able to hear Him, speak His words, do His works, and fulfill His will. He gave us the Holy Spirit to instruct and help us, to be in us and with us (see John 14:17). We have His inward witness and His grace upon us. When you consecrate yourself to Him "as a holy and living sacrifice" (Romans 12:1), aligning your thoughts and your actions with His purposes, His right way of doing things, you will experience God's life-changing power that transforms you. We need to think more on God's ways—and His righteousness, His right way of doing things by His Spirit. Jesus commands,

> But seek first the kingdom of God and His righteousness, and all these things will be provided for you. (Matthew 6:33 HCSB)

Being in right relationship with God does not mean that you will not face temptation. The opposite is true. Paul personifies sin in the flesh: "But I see another law in my members, warring against the law of my mind" (Romans 7:23). But we also face outside assaults on our minds from the enemy. Don't believe every thought originated in your mind. The battle for control of your mind is won in meditating and speaking His Word, consecration, and faith in God's grace. God will do His part; and your part is to yield to His action within you, and replace wrong thoughts with His thoughts.

As well as causing wrong thoughts, the enemy tries to imitate the voice of the Holy Spirit. Get to know the voice of the Holy Spirit. The Holy Spirit, your inward witness, will help you detect the enemy's wiles. One way to begin to recognize his voice is by communing with Him in His Word daily.

## Scripture Meditation

But we have the mind of Christ (the Messiah) and do hold the thoughts (feelings and purposes) of His heart. (1 Corinthians 2:16 AMP)

## A Renewed Mind is Gifted with Wisdom

In every circumstance, decision or dilemma, know that you have within you the wisdom of God to know the right way to go and act. If you have filled and are continually filling your mind and spirit with the Word of God, which contains His wisdom, then you have His ways. Further, you have an anointing on the inside to teach you. Writes John, "But you have an anointing from the Holy One, and you all know. As for you, the anointing which you received from Him abides in you, and you have no need for anyone to teach you; but as His anointing teaches you about all things, and is true and is not a lie, and just as it has taught you, you abide in Him" (1 John 2:20,27).

Replace any thought of confusion with God's thoughts about you. If you are facing a decision, and you do not have a conscious answer, then do nothing. If you must take action without an answer, know that God can find you, even if you make a wrong turn. He puts desires in your heart; follow them. Let your peace be the compass that you follow—that inward witness. If you lack, then ask of God. When you ask, you can have the wisdom from above. "The wisdom from above is pure, then peaceable . . . " (James 3:17).

> *Let your peace be the compass that you follow—that inward witness.*

> For everyone who asks receives, and the one who searches finds, and to the one who knocks, the door will be opened. (Matthew 7:8 HCSB)

Jesus is "made unto us wisdom from God," according to Paul's letter to the Corinthian church. When Jesus Christ is your Lord, you have all you need. He is your wisdom. He is the Great Repository for all we need. Paul exclaims, "In Him are hidden all the treasures of wisdom and knowledge" (Colossians 2:3).

### Scripture Meditation

But it is from Him that you have your life in Christ Jesus, Whom God made our Wisdom from God . . . (1 Corinthians 1:30)

## You Are Moment By Moment Being
## Transformed As You Behold The Word in His Presence

Think on these promises in the Word: You have the mind of Christ (1 Corinthians 2:16). You are united with Him in one spirit (1 Corinthians 6:17. You are being transformed more and more into His image as you think on His thoughts in the Word of God (Romans 12:2). You are being transformed into His image as you behold Him in the Word ((2 Corinthians 3:18). Ask the Holy Spirit to bring revelation on your transformation. As the moon reflects the sun, we reflect the light of the gospel, the glory of God on the face of Christ, and grow brighter and brighter with each moment in His Presence. This is a work of the Holy Spirit, not our works. We merely cooperate by staying in His Word, being transformed, fashioned, into the same image we reflect.

God is building the image of His Son in you, bringing you to the glory to be revealed when Christ is revealed in His glory at the end of this age. The veil over Moses' face was to cover the fading glory (see 2 Corinthians 3:13). The glory of God on the face of Christ, which you reflect, is eternal (see 2 Corinthians 4:6). Bask in it daily, and watch your life and character be transformed. The glory you experience in His Presence will transform you so greatly, you will become more like Him in what you think, say and do.

> *The glory of God on the face of Christ, which you reflect, is eternal.*

Patience and perseverance are other words for endurance. We can expect, as we persevere in the Word, and endure any tribulation joyfully, to begin to possess godly character. Paul encourages the Romans, "Endurance produces proven character, and proven character produces hope" (Romans 5:4). Hope manifests as we begin to see changes in our lives—Christ formed in us (see Galatians 4:19). It takes both faith and patience to possess all God has for us in Christ, to "inherit the promises through faith and perseverance"(Hebrews 6:12).

### Scripture Meditation

And all of us, with our unveiled faces like mirrors reflecting the glory of the Lord, are being transformed into the image that we reflect in brighter and brighter glory; this is the working of the Lord who is the Spirit. ( 2 Corinthians 3:18)

# You Have Life, Peace, and Joy

The old self allowed thoughts of sin and also condemnation. The old self allowed the mind to run amuck without a guard over it, indulging self-pity or thoughts of rejection and bitterness. But the renewed mind and attitude in the Spirit keeps peace and an inflow of life by thinking and acting in accordance with the Word of God. Righteousness, joy and peace in the Holy Spirit are characteristics of the Kingdom of God (see Romans 14:17). If you are not in peace, then you are not in faith. Reset your faith and peace compass; "The God of Hope will fill you with joy and peace in believing" (Romans 15:13). Faith, joy and peace go hand in hand. We should have joy in believing God (faith), and peace is a manifestation of God's Presence.

Check your mind-set frequently. Are you dwelling on thoughts that minister life, and looking at images that minister life to you or images and thoughts producing death? It is your choice. What you feed will grow. You will gravitate toward what you dwell on in your mind, and produce in your life the vision that you hold. The law of sowing and reaping works not only regarding finances, but life in general. When you spend time in the Word of God, you are sowing to life. The Holy Spirit is able to minister life to you. In a similar manner, when you are caught up in circumstances and world issues, you are not ministering life but corruption. "The one who sows to the flesh will reap corruption, but the one who sows to the Spirit will reap eternal life from the Spirit (Galatians 6:8 HCSB).

We often fail to honor and serve God with a joyful heart for all He had given us. God warned the Israelites to serve Him with rejoicing; in fact, He warned they would be expelled from the Promised Land. Moses says:

> Because you didn't serve the LORD your God with joy
> and a cheerful heart, even though you had an abundance
> of everything. (Deuteronomy 28:47)

## Scripture Meditation

Now the mind of the flesh [which is sense and reason without the Holy Spirit] is death [death that comprises all the miseries arising from sin, both here and hereafter]. But the mind of the [Holy] Spirit is life and [soul] peace [both now and forever]. (Romans 8:6 AMP)

## You Are Holy, SoThink Holy Thoughts

Bad thoughts create negative energy in your body and a negative attitude. Foremost, God wants us to manifest the joy Jesus died to give us. Jesus said, "I have spoken these things to you so that My joy may be in you and your joy may be complete" (John 15:11). Laughter is good medicine (see Proverbs 17:22).

When Satan brings thoughts of failure or unworthiness, change them. Fill your mind with thoughts on your righteousness and holiness provided by God through Christ. Quit trying to measure your self-worth based on your standards or another's, and on your performance—that only leads to perfectionism, a sense of rejection and failure—and ultimately fear of failure. Believe what God says about your value. Meditate on the fact that you are holy. You have been chosen and set apart by God, consecrated for His purpose. Paul encourages us, "And whom He predestined, these He also called, and whom He called, these He also justified, whom He justified, these He also glorified" (Romans 8:30).

Your justification and glorification are a sure thing in union with Christ. God has not withheld anything from you, in fact, " . . . for all things belong to you" (1 Corinthians 3:21). Keep His thoughts of goodness toward you on your mind and heart. Remember you have only two kinds of thoughts; because you are in union with Christ, you have God's thoughts or the enemy's thoughts. Purpose to replace any thoughts that are not of God. A simple formula will help you; good thoughts are God's thoughts, and bad thoughts are Satan's thoughts.

When tempted to dwell on failures or mistakes, just remember that you cannot fail, if you do not quit! Your perseverance brings victory. David said of his mind, "I will keep the LORD in mind always. Because He is at my right hand, I will not be shaken" (Psalm 16:8 HCSB). Do not be moved by unrighteous thoughts that are not yours. Turn your thoughts to the Lord, and rest in Him. Jesus said, "My peace I leave with you" (John 14:27).

## Scripture Meditation

But by His doing you are in Christ Jesus, Who became to us Wisdom from God, and Righteousness, and Sanctification, and Redemption. (1 Corinthians 1:30)

# Keep Yourself Clean

Your mind and spirit can become contaminated. You are responsible to avoid opening yourself to harmful inflows that can contaminate and defile. You have been made righteous, upright before God, but it is your responsibility to keep yourself from things that defile. Accepting and thinking on the wrong thoughts, watching the wrong things and speaking the wrong words can cause your mind to become a receptacle for the devil's trash. The devil's thoughts are seeds that form roots and work against you if they are not immediately uprooted. Knowing you are righteous, that the Holy Spirit dwells within, realize wrong thoughts

> *The devil's thoughts are seeds form root s and work against you if they are not immediately uprooted.*

are not of God, and immediately reject them before they can produce a bad harvest in you. Since you are righteous and in union with Christ, your thoughts are righteous or they are from the devil. Do not keep His thoughts. Do not believe every thought that enters your mind, even if in the first person.

Visual images give rise to thoughts. King David said, "I will set no evil before my eyes" (Psalm 101:3). The wisdom of Proverbs reads, "Guard your heart, out of it flow the issues of life" (the borders and boundaries) (Proverbs 4:22). Keep a tight reign on your eyes and ears and actions. In other words, guard your thoughts, tongue, and ears. James writes, "Be quick to hear, slow to speak, and slow to anger" (James 1:19). Anger is a door for the enemy if you act on it.

What you fellowship with will eventually manifest out of your mouth. Stay clean by keeping your heart clean. Jesus said, "For the mouth speaks from the overflow of the heart (Matthew 12:34 HCSB). You are fellowshipping with the spirit of whatever is behind what you put your mind on. Is it God or His Word, or something altogether different? It is up to you to walk holy in fellowship with the Holy Spirit, and cleanse yourself if you come into contact with uncleaness.

## Scripture Meditation

Therefore since these [great] promises are ours, beloved, let us cleanse ourselves from everything that contaminates and defiles body and spirit, and bring [our] consecration to completeness in the [reverential] fear of God]. (2 Corinthians 7:1 AMP)

## Thinking and Speaking The Word Is
## Satan's Defeat

The enemy may work on a believer for a long time, patiently trying to get his wrong thoughts and beliefs to take root. His objective is to have you live a life of defeat and give up on God. Thoughts and words create reality. The right thoughts connected with the right words create power. Wrong

> *Thoughts and words create reality.*

thoughts and wrong words will create weakness, defeat, sickness and depression. You become what you behold (2 Corinthians 3:18). You attract and gravitate toward what you keep before you.

Words will propel you in the direction they are aimed. They are containers of power. Change your thoughts and your words, and change your reality. You will need to interrupt bad thoughts and align them with the Word of God. Put good things in your heart with the Word. Jesus said, "The good man out of the good treasure of his heart bringeth forth that which is good; and the evil (man) out of the evil (treasure) bringeth forth that which is evil" (Luke 6:4). Give your High Priest faith-filled words; "Consider Jesus, the Apostle and High Priest of our confession" (Hebrews 2:1). Our words are so very important. They will establish our course and be used in eternity. Jesus warned against unfounded (idle) words. Words can be used for us or against us.

The Holy Spirit is using the Word of God that you put into your heart to build a beautiful portrait of who you are in Christ. Satan wants to destroy this portrait. Arm yourself with this knowledge. Defeat the enemy with the sword of the Spirit, the spoken Word of God (Ephesians 6:17). It is a living Word and will produce life, or it will cut through like a sword and destroy (see Hebrews 4:12).

### Scripture Meditation

So I tell you this, that for every unfounded word people utter they will answer on Judgment Day, since it is by your words you will be justified, and by your words condemned. (Matthew 12:36-37)

## Set Your Mind On God, Your Rock

You cannot stay focused on the greatness of God, and at the same time get into doubt and unbelief. Trust God to keep you. If you miss the mark, then trust Him to forgive you and set you on the right path. You will "set your mind" by meditating on scripture revealing God's faithfulness.

God promises that we have peace; He is the God of peace (Hebrews 13:20). Jesus is the Prince of Peace (Isaiah 9:6). He gave us His peace (John 14:27). When you focus on Him, He inspires confidence and peace. Inspired by the Spirit of God, David said, "Those who love Thy law have great peace" ( Psalm 119:165). Isaiah writes, "He will keep in perfect peace whose mind is staid on Thee; because he trusts in Thee" (Isaiah 26:3). Your peace will be fixed when your heart is fixed on God—and He is our Rock.

David was on the run from King Saul for a number of years, hiding in caves and even pretending insanity to escape death. Only one thing kept him trusting in the promise that he would one day be king. He set His eyes on God. He wrote, "My eyes are continually toward the Lord, for He will pluck my feet out of the net" (Psalm 25:15). God will not fail us. He said that He would never leave us, and that we can say the Lord is our helper (see Hebrews 13:5b-6).

We must keep our eyes on Him at all times. We cannot be looking backward and also looking at the Lord our Rock. We will lose sight of the goal. It has been said, chase two rabbits and you will lose both of them. Paul proclaimed that he stretched forward and did one thing:

> But one thing I do: forgetting what is behind and reaching forward to what is ahead, I pursue as my goal the prize promised by God's heavenly call in Christ Jesus. (Philippians 3:13-14 HCSB)

### Scripture Meditation

. . . The one that remains faithful, the steadfast of mind Thou shalt keep in perfect peace because his mind is staid on Thee. Trust in the Lord forever, for in God the Lord, we have an everlasting Rock. (Isaiah 26:2-4)

# Have a Mind-Set of Faith

A mind-set of faith is an attitude, a purposeful decision to trust God in every circumstance, to believe in His grace and goodness. Your fight is to stay in faith and avoid looking at circumstances instead of the promises of God. You come out of faith when you begin to look at yourself, your circumstances, and your life instead of looking at God. You only doubt when you look at yourself apart from God's greatness and promises. Your mind-set will determine how you respond to any given situation. Have a mind-set of faith and victory.

Develop a spirit of faith that says, "I am well able to possess what God has given me in Christ." You will be imitating some heroes of faith. In Numbers 13, Moses sent out twelve spies to reconnoiter the Promised Land. Ten came back with negative reports, "It's a good land but we saw ourselves as grasshoppers in the sight of the natives" (Numbers 13:33 Paraphrase). These ten spies let the circumstances determine how they saw themselves and their future. But two of the spies, Joshua and Caleb, who saw the same land and the same inhabitants, gave a different report. They had a mind-set of faith in God. Caleb said, "We are well able to possess the land for God

> *Do not become a grasshopper in your own sight*

has given it to us" (Numbers 13:30 paraphrase). They took God at His word. If you hear yourself whine or complain, then you are not in faith. Keep at it! Put a tone of victory in your voice. Faith speaks the Word of God, the word of faith. Do not become a grasshopper in your own sight. If you fear failure, then your standard of measure is not God's. Self-confidence comes from knowing the Greater One in you, who He is in you and what He has done for you. His promises are sure. He is your Father, after all. He made His kids to be like Him.

At eighty-five years of age, Caleb was strong and still full of faith. He asked Joshua to give him the hill country where the giants lived and where fortified cities were established, so he could possess what the Lord had promised. He honored God with his faith, wanting to fulfill what the Lord had said Israel could do forty-five years earlier.

## Scripture Meditation

But having the same spirit of faith, according to what is written, "I believed, therefore I spoke," we also believe, therefore we also speak. (2 Corinthians 4:13)

# Do Not Tolerate A Mind-Set of Fear

A person with a mind-set of fear allows the enemy to exercise his influence. Fear is based on the belief that you do not have what it takes to meet a circumstance. A fear mind-set places more trust in the enemy than in the Lord. Faith empowers you in God's kingdom. Conversely, fear empowers the negative in your life to occur. Once fear gains a foothold, it will move into every area until it pervades one's life. A person with a mind-set of fear will avoid faith situations and even cease to take risks for advancement, fearing failure. This person is looking at their worth based on their performance and fear of not performing acceptably to themselves or others. Instead embrace the Holy Spirit's empowerment. Faith accesses God's grace and empowerment.

Your faith and boldness is based on what you believe about yourself—what God has said about your righteousness through Christ. Proverbs reveals, "The wicked flee when no one is pursuing, but the righteous are as bold as a lion" (Proverbs 28:1).

Fear paralyzes, but faith mobilizes. Fear shrinks back at the promises of God, but faith pursues and embraces the promises of God. If you have found yourself in fear, break free with meditation on God's protection and provision. Fear will try to come, but refuse it. Someone said, "Fear came and knocked at the door, but Faith answered the knock, and no one was there." Fear has to be faced and defeated with confidence.

Speak words of faith against fear. Strengthen yourself in the Word and prayer. Praying in the Spirit will charge your spiritual batteries and bring victory. Jude writes, "Build yourself up on your most holy faith, praying in the Spirit" (Jude 20). Remind your self that God's Spirit is with you and in you (see John 14:17).

I like to say with Paul, "Such confidence we have toward God through Christ (2 Corinthians 3:4). This is a confidence that comes in and through relationship—in knowing God is competent, not us, and He is with us and in us!

## Scripture Meditation

For God did not give us a spirit of timidity (of cowardice, of craven and cringing and fawning fear), but [He has given us a spirit] of power and of love and of calm and well-balanced mind and discipline and self-control. (2 Timothy 1:7 AMP)

# Raise Your Faith To A New Level

The written Word of God, *logos* in Greek, becomes the *Rhema* Word of God, when the Spirit of God quickens it or speaks it. The Lord Jesus is the living Word. Put the *Rhema* Word in your mouth, think and speak (meditate) it, and you will be releasing power for the living Word in your life. You can propel yourself and build a bigger faith shield (see Ephesians 6) for your life by speaking power Words from the Biblical text.

Your faith will grow by hearing the Word. The Bible says, "Faith comes by hearing and hearing by the Word of Christ" (Romans 10:17). Therefore, more Word will produce more faith! You can expand the very borders and boundaries of your life by the Word you place in your heart and mouth. The formula is found in the words of Jesus, "Out of the abundance of the heart, the mouth speaks" (Luke 6:45). You will free yourself or imprison yourself, based on the thoughts and words you allow. Solomon expounds, "A man's belly shall be satisfied with the fruit of his mouth; [and] with the increase of his lips shall he be filled" (Proverbs 18:20).

The woman who had an issue of blood for twelve years kept saying to herself that she would be healed if only she touched the tassels of Jesus' garment (the *Tzitzit*–the twisted and knotted coils of His prayer shawl). As she spoke over and over, her faith began to build. Finally, she pressed in and merely touched the *Tzitzit* of His prayer shawl. Healing virtue (power) flowed from Jesus for her healing (see Matthew 9:20). The Israelites called the *Tzitzit* on the corners of their prayer shawls "wings." This woman knew from the Scriptures that "the Sun of Righteousness would rise with healing in His wings" (Malachi 4:2). Propelled by her words, her perseverance and faith in Jesus the Messiah brought wholeness in her life. "Have courage, daughter," He said. "Your faith has made you well" (Matthew 9:22).

## Scripture Meditation

[Let] the high [praises] of God [be] in their mouth, and a twoedged sword in their hand. (Psalm 149:6 AMP)

## Know That God Is Trustworthy, and
## You Must Stay On His Side

When you do not understand why a difficulty or new trial has come into your life, continue to trust God to bring you through it. Your own imagination may envision any number of reasons for the circumstance, chiefly focusing on your failures. Trust the Holy Spirit to reveal any error. Avoid pointing a finger at yourself or at God, questioning His goodness toward you. You will not succeed or overcome by asking, "Why me?" or even, "What did I do to deserve this?" Satan wants you to focus on yourself. It is only when you look at yourself that you consider failure. But if you will keep your thoughts and your words in line with the goodness of God, staying on His side, then you will come through victoriously.

If you have truly grasped your righteousness in Christ Jesus, then you know by now that bad thoughts are not from God, but Satan. God is at work to bring about your good. You can trust Him. He has good thoughts toward you (see Jeremiah 29:11).

God and His Word are one. He will fulfill it. The Psalmist loved the Word so much that he even praised the Word of God (Psalm 56:4. 10, 138:2). God watches over His Word to perform it (Jeremiah 1:12). If you receive His Word for what it is, it will do a mighty work in you. Paul writes, "When you received from us the word of God, you received it not as the word of men, but, as it is

> *When the Word of God is at work in you, it is God at work in you.*

in truth, the word of God, which also performs its work in you that believe" (1 Thessalonians 2:13). When the Word of God is at work in you, it is God at work in you.

God promises to lead you out of any bad circumstance—to provide a way of escape and a safe landing (see 1 Corinthians 10:13).

### Scripture Meditation

. . . Work out your salvation with fear and trembling; for it is God who is at work in you both to will and to work for His good pleasure (Philippians 2:12-13)

# You Are in The
# Occupation Force!

The Lord Jesus Christ won a mighty victory for you. He defeated the enemy through the cross. You are now a child of God, made righteous through Christ. As a new creation, born from above, you are at peace with God (John 3:16, Romans 5:1) and endued with the ability of God,when you are baptized in the Holy Spirit (Acts 2:8). Your must remember that Christ won your peace; you just enforce it much as an occupation army enforces the peace in a conquered land. You must possess the promises of God in the Word. Until you meditate on them, get them in your heart, and speak them, they will not become a reality in your life.

King Jehosaphat had only to seek God before the battle against a superior force, and then show up for the battle to win it. He positioned the Levites to praise God in front of the army, and God won the victory for them. The Chronicler writes, "The battle is not yours but the LORD's" ( 2 Chronicles 20:15). Your battle is won because Jesus won the victory over the enemy, and you are in Him. Yes, He won the victory

> *very*
> *"Life is* ^ *good."*

for us; we need only enforce the victory until He returns. God defeated Satan through Christ, who humiliated Satan—"made a show of him openly" (Colossians 2:15).

Manage your time well and allow time to enforce your victory over any force attempting to come against you. We are made "more than conquerors" in Christ. One translation calls us super conquerors (Romans 8:37). We are overwhelmingly victorious through Christ.

Jesus said, "Occupy until I come" (Luke 19:13). While here, enjoy the good life God gave us through Christ, "life and life abundantly" (John 10:10). Life is not just good, so begin to say,

**very**
**"Life is ^ good."**

## Scripture Meditation

Blotting out the handwriting of ordinances that was against us, which was contrary to us, and took it out of the way, nailing it to the cross; God spoiled principalities and powers; He made a show of them openly, triumphing over them in it. (Colossians 2:14-15)

## Think And Speak Like
## The Redeemed Of God


King David knew persecution. He was on the run for seven years from King Saul. Many times he reveals his cries to God for help in the Psalms. Yet he also wrote, "Let the redeemed of the Lord say so" (Psalm 107:2). You are the redeemed of the Lord; say so. Speak that you are redeemed from spiritual death, the curse of the law, poverty, sickness, and that you have been removed to safety. Paul boldly says, "Having the same spirit of faith, I believed, therefore I spoke" (2 Corinthians 4:13). Think and speak on your redemption. You did not just receive fire insurance when you made Jesus Christ Lord of your life, but you received all the benefits of His riches in glory for this life!

As you feed your spirit from the soul's healthy food (knowledge and understanding of your status in redemption), it will produce health. If you feed your spirit bad food, it will produce dis-order and dis-ease. Much like a computer, what you put in your heart determines what you get out. If you run it according to the Manufacturer's design, using the right software, then you will have good success. Program it (your heart) for good. Live in accordance with the revelation in your spirit, and you will walk in freedom with a renewed mind, a healthy body, and success in life. Jesus said,

> For the mouth speaks out of that which fills the heart.
> The good man brings out of good treasure what is good,
> and the evil man brings out of evil treasure what is evil.
> (Matthew 12:34b-35)

John prays by the Spirit, that we have prosperity and be in health (3 John 2). It means to have wholeness, soundness, and all one needs for life.

### Scripture Meditation

Beloved I pray you prosper and be in health as your soul prospers. (1 John 3:2)

# Guilty or Forgiven?

Many are confused about forgiveness and righteousness. Not understanding, they lump all sin and resulting feelings of condemnation into one basket; i.e., you committed a sin and therefore you are guilty. Not so. You are free to speak of God's forgiveness, and push away feelings of guilt since you now have been made righteous!

Guilt was in place, and rightly so, condemnation, before you received knowledge of Christ's work on your behalf. You may have experienced guilt marked by pressure, a sense of being separate from God and aloneness. If not for that knowledge of sin and guilt, and conviction by the Holy Spirit, you would not have repented, been converted, and received forgiveness and righteous by the faith of Jesus Christ.

> *Pressure and a sense of guilt are not from God—that characterized the old man's life. A gentle tug or conviction is from the Holy Spirit, and of the new man's life.*

Now, since you are set-right-with-God through Christ, meaning that you are justified and declared righteous, you experience conviction by your own conscience and by the gentle tug of the Holy Spirit if you miss-the-mark.

Remember, pressure and a sense of guilt are not from God—that characterized the old man's life. A gentle tug or conviction is from the Holy Spirit, and of the new man's life. Having peace with God through Christ, we can recognize missing the mark and immediately, repent, and be cleansed, never wallowing in guilt. I like to apologize to God if I miss it, just as I would to an earthly father. But God, being so much greater, grants not only forgiveness, but also cleansing.

Just like Father Abraham, we believe God, what He did for us through the faith of Jesus Christ, and God calls us redeemed! We are declared righteous, set-right-with-God, and God grants us sonship.

## Scripture Meditation

And he believed! Believed GOD! God declared him "Set-Right-with-God." (Genesis 15:6 MSG)

41

# Your Faith is More Precious Than Pure Gold

When gold is purified, it goes through intense heat. The impurities in it rise to the surface to be skimmed off. You will be shown the purity of your heart and your faith through the trials that come upon you. They may be fiery ones. This is the crucible. How else will you grow if your faith is not put to the test? Peter wrote to those experiencing grief due to trials and severe persecution,

> Even though now for a season, if necessary, you have been distressed by various trials, that the genuineness of your faith, more precious than gold tested by fire, which is perishable, may result in praise, glory and honor at the revelation of Jesus Christ. (1 Peter 1:6-7)

In the midst of the trial, you may not see or hear from God, but He is at work nonetheless. He is faithful. Job cried, "But He knows the way I take—when He has tested me, I shall come forth as gold" (Job 23:10). Solomon wrote, "Take away dross from silver and it comes forth for the refiner" (Proverbs 25:4).

It is good to know that God takes a personal interest in seeing that we make it through the trials. He stands with us, and He personally sees to it that we are "restored, more firmly rooted, supported, and strengthened" (1 Peter 5:10). It is important that you keep seeking God in the midst of any trial, and seek His purpose in it. He will bring you forth as gold. If you cleave to Him in love, and learn to know Him, then He will (1) deliver you, (2) answer you, (3) be with you in trouble, (4) rescue you and honor you, and (5) with long life satisfy you and let you see His salvation (Psalm 91:14-16).

## Scripture Meditation

Now the God of all grace, who called you to His eternal glory in Christ Jesus, will personally perfect, restore, confirm, establish, strengthen and support you after you have suffered a little. (1 Peter 5:10 paraphrase)

## You Are Not Alone

In the midst of any test or trial, you must remember that the Lord is with you. He has suffered and knows what you are going through. He is not far awar, but "in all their affliction, He was afflicted" (Isaiah 63:9). He does not leave you alone. Satan wants you to believe that no one has ever suffered as you have, and that you are totally alone in your trial whether one of secrecy or shared with the Body of Christ. But the Lord tells us through the Apostle Paul,

> *Remember, if you cleave to Him in love, and learn to know Him, then He will (1) deliver you, (2) answer you, (3) be with you in trouble, (4) rescue you and honor you, and (5) with long life satisfy you and let you see His salvation.*
> *(Psalm 91:14-16)*

No temptation (test or trial) has overtaken you but such as is common to man, and God is faithful, who will not allow you to be tempted beyond what you are able, but with the temptation will provides a way to escape it that you may endure it. (1 Corinthians 10:13)

We have a Divine Helper, One who bends down, and condescends to help us. We are in His hands. Jesus reminded His followers that every hair on our heads is numbered, that not even a sparrow falls to the ground that God does not know about, and that no one can pluck us out of the Father's hands (Matthew 10:29, 30, John 10:29). In trials, attacks, infirmities, remind yourself that nothing (no one) can separate you from the love of God in Christ Jesus (Romans 8:39).

## Scripture Meditation

For He Himself has said, "(I will) not, (I will) not, (I will) not in any degree leave you helpless not forsake nor let (you) down," so that we can boldly say, the Lord is my Helper, I will not fear what man can do to me." (Hebrews 13: 5-6 AMP)

## Fasting Prayer—A Weapon in Your Arsenal

Your faith expands as you pursue and rest in God's Presence. It is in intense pursuit that you will make the most advances in your knowledge of and intimacy with God. Fasting with Prayer is a method to intensify your pursuit. I call it "fasting prayer" (See Living the Fasted Life, by Dr. Shirley Christian). Fasting definitely helps to loosen the world's hold as you daily put to death your physical desire for food, and allow your spiritual desire toward God to soar. Andrew Murray wrote, "Faith requires both prayer and fasting. That is, prayer grasps the power of heaven, and fasting loosens the hold on earthy pleasure." While you may not pray every minute of the day during a fast, you remain in a "fasting state of prayer." This term, fasting prayer, is the best way that I can describe "how you are with God" during a fast. When you are longing for as much of God as you can have, fasting prayer gives you that edge to prayer and pursuit.

If you have never fasted for any length of time, begin slowly, missing a few meals and praying. Then begin to progress to longer times of fasting prayer. God will provide the grace for all you do in pursuit of Him.

Your sense of righteousness, your right standing with God, must be experienced before you are comfortable in asking God in prayer for all your needs. Your faith and righteousness are inseparable. While you are made righteous through the faith of Jesus, He expects your personal faith to grow and appropriate all that He died to make possible for you. You must pursue Him in faith, believing that He will reward your efforts. Time is His Presence is never wasted.

## Scripture Meditation

Without faith, it is impossible to please God, for He who comes to God must believe that He is, and that He is a rewarder of those who seek Him (Hebrews 11:6).

## Progress Toward True Knowledge

The more your mind is renewed in the image of God, your Creator, the more you will progress in the new man. If you feel powerless in your efforts to put away sin and the past (the old man), then be encouraged. You have arrived to the point where God can complete His work in you. Once you cease in your own efforts, His grace is at full stretch. He is the Empowerer.

God sees the light in you. Jesus said, "You are the light of the world" (Matthew 5:14). He will preserve and perfect His own. Paul writes to Timothy, "The Lord knows those who are His own" (2 Timothy 2:9). David said, "The LORD will accomplish what concerns me" (Psalm 138:8a). Your part is to do what you know to do: renew your mind in the Word, and be a doer of the Word (Romans 12:2, James 1:22). God's part is the transformation. You are transformed from a weak fleshly-ruled person to a mighty spirit-ruled person. You have the help of the Holy Spirit in doing your part. John says, "Greater is He in you than he that is in the world" (1 John 4:4).

> *The LORD will accomplish what concerns me.*
> *(Psalm 138:8a)*

As you are renewing your mind, and being molded into the image of Christ, you see sin and its consequences in light of true knowledge. You are more aware of the enemy's tactics to bring back darkness, but you know that "You are light in the Lord" (Ephesians 5:8). Being light, you will walk in the Light, where you have fellowship and the blood of Jesus, God's Son, cleanses you from all sin (see 1 John 1:7).

## Scripture Meditation

. . . the wealth that comes from the full assurance of understanding, a true knowledge of God's mystery, Christ, in whom are hidden all the treasures of wisdom and knowledge. (Colossians 2:2-3)

## A Heart of Thanksgiving

Jeremiah prophesied of "The Lord our Righteousness" (Jeremiah 23:6). If all believers would grasp this precious gift of God and see their perfection in Christ, a heart of thanksgiving would emerge. Paul sums our need and result: "We proclaim Him, warning and teaching everyone with all wisdom, so that we may present everyone perfect in Christ" (Colossians 1:28). Again, Paul tells us that it is by Christ that we are made perfect, not by our having perfect lives: "Not having mine own righteousness, which is of the law, but that which is through the faith of Christ, the righteousness which is of God by faith." By the faith of Christ, we see that God made us righteous, and then we rejoice in God's goodness. Our gratitude in these things moves us to love Him greatly, and serve Him whole-heartedly. Since Christ died for us, how much more should we die to our selfishness and live for Him in constant gratitude.

> *You can only reach your true destiny in this life and eternity through your true identity in Christ*

"And He died for all so that those who live should no longer live for themselves, but for the One who died for them and was raised" (2 Corinthians 5:15).

Charles Spurgeon writes of this great sense of gratitude and motivation, "When the believer says, "I live on Christ alone; I rest on him solely for salvation; and I believe that, however unworthy, I am still saved in Jesus;" then there rises up as a motive of gratitude this thought-"Shall I not live to Christ? Shall I not love him and serve him, seeing that I am saved by his merits?"

You can only reach your true destiny in this life and eternity through your true identity in Christ. You have entered God's rest (Hebrews 4:3) when you take on your true identity that He provided in Christ. Then in love and gratitude, serve Him by serving others.

## Scripture Meditation

I no longer live, but Christ lives in me. The life I now live in the flesh, I live by faith of the Son of God, who loved me and gave Himself for me. (Galatians 2:20)

# BIBLIOGRAPHY

Unless otherwise indicated, all scripture is from the <u>New American Standard Bible</u>, copyright 1960, 1962, 1963, 1968, 1971,1972, 1973, 1975, 1977, 1995 by th3 Lockman Foundation, Used by Permission.

Scripture references marked AMP are from the <u>Amplified Bible</u>, Old Testament copyright 1965, 1987 by the Zondervan Corporation. The Amplified New Testament copyright 1958, 1987 by the Lockman Foundation 1958-1987. Used by permisison.

<u>Holman Christian Standard Bible (HCSB)</u>, Nashville Tennesee. Homan Bible Publishers 2000. Used by permission.

<u>New International Version</u> (NIV). Copyright © 1973, 1978, 1984 by <u>International Bible Society.</u> Used by Permission.

Peterson, Eugene. <u>Message Bible (MSG)</u>. Navpress: Copyright © 1993, 1994, 1995, 1996, 2000, 2001, 2002. Used by permission.

<u>New Living Translation</u> (NLT) Holy Bible. Copyright © 1996, 2004 by Tyndale Charitable Trust. Used by permission of Tyndale House Publishers. Used by Permission.


Stern, David. <u>Jewish New Testament</u> (JNT): Jewish New Testament Publications, Inc , Clarksville, Maryland, 1979. Used by permission.

# ABOUT THE AUTHOR

Dr. Shirley Christian actively fulfills a role of instruction and oversight as Professor of Biblical Studies at a Bible School in Lubbock, Texas. Her many years of ministry in a healing school with the gifts of the Spirit in operation, and the things she had gone through personally, worked a deep compassion within her for the lost and hurting. The Holy Spirit entrusted Shirley with a strong intercessory prayer life, healing and prophetic giftings, and through her brings truth and deliverance to the Body of Christ. Shirley flows in streams of His grace, streams of intercession, cleansing, healing and revelation.

The Holy Spirit inspired the motto, Streams of His Grace, for Shirley Christian Ministries during a time of prayer. Shirley believes the inspiration for the motto is based on how the Holy Spirit manifests His presence in streams of revelation, power and intercession.

If you enjoyed <u>Keys to a Sound Mind</u> by Dr. Shirley Christian, please visit the ministry website for other products and books such as <u>Types and Shadows, Prophetic Pictures of Wholeness in Christ</u>, <u>Living the Fasted Life,</u> and <u>Cleansing and Healing Streams</u>. You will also find free downloads of teaching and confession CDS on her ministry website:

<u>www.shirleychristian.org</u>

www.ingramcontent.com/pod-product-compliance
Lightning Source LLC
Chambersburg PA
CBHW031335040426
42443CB00005B/348